SYSTEMS FIRST $CALE FAST

SYSTEMS FIRST $CALE FAST

Pavan Verma
CRM & ERP Systems Expert

Available on amazonkindle

Worldwide Published by

Pendown Press
PREMIUM BUSINESS PUBLISHER

PENDOWN PRESS LLP

An ISO 9001 & ISO 14001 Certified Co.,

Regd. Office: 3767A, Kanhaiya Nagar,
Tri Nagar, Delhi-110035
Ph.: 8130886000, 9650072927
E-mail: info@pendownpress.com
Branch Office: 1A/2A, 20, Hari Sadan, Ansari Road,
Daryaganj, New Delhi-110002
Ph.: 011-45794768
Website: PendownPress.com

Edition: 2025
Price: ₹ 499
ISBN: 978-93-6338-728-7

Layout and Cover Designed by Pendown Graphics Team
Printed and Bound in India by Thomson Press India Ltd.

Dedication

This book is dedicated to every business owner who has chosen the path of entrepreneurship, a journey filled with uncertainties, struggles, and silent battles. I salute your courage, your resilience, and your relentless pursuit of your dreams.

Through this book, my mission is to help business owners break free from operational chaos, build strong systems, and shift their focus toward growth. Because you deserve to work on your vision, not just in your business.

To all the dreamers, doers, and believers, this one's for you.

To the Dreamers, the Doers, the Decision Makers

You chose a path of passion and drive,
Building a dream, making it thrive.

Big ideas, a vision so clear,
Yet the day-to-day pulls you near.

Endless tasks, the hustle, the race,
Wearing too many hats, keeping the pace.

But what if growth didn't feel this way?
What if chaos no longer ruled your day?

With the right Systems, strong and true,
Your business flows, your dreams shine through.

No more fire-fighting, no more delay,
Focus on growth, let nothing sway.

So step ahead, take back control,
Let Business Systems support, let efficiency roll.

Build, scale, and watch it grow,
With clarity and ease, let your business flow.

SCALABLE
GROWTH &
EFFICIENCY
SMART
SYSTEMS

Contents

Preface

Running a business is not easy. I have seen it, lived it, and struggled through it, just like you probably have. Sleepless nights, endless to-do lists, and the constant feeling that no matter how hard you work, something is always slipping through your hands.

This book comes from that same place.

Not from a big office or a fancy boardroom. But from real conversations, real failures, and real wins. I have spoken to many business owners who felt stuck, tired of handling everything on their own, unsure of what is going wrong, and just wishing for some peace and clarity.

I do not claim to have all the answers. But I do have a deep desire to help you make things simpler. To clear the confusion. To show you that there is a better way to run your business without burning yourself out.

This book is written in simple words.

It is not for experts or technical people.

It is for people like us, hardworking, passionate, and sometimes just needing someone to say, I understand what you are going through, and I am here to help.

If you are holding this book right now, I just want to say thank you.

Thank you for trusting me. Thank you for choosing to take the first step.

Now let us begin this journey together.

With respect and honesty
Pavan Verma

Acknowledgement

This book is not just a collection of words – it is a journey, one that I could not have walked alone. It is a reflection of the love, wisdom, and support I have received from so many incredible people in my life.

To my **parents, Late Mr. Subhash Verma and Dr. Shanti Verma,** your unwavering love, guidance, and wisdom have shaped me into the person I am today. Every step I take is built on the foundation of your teachings, and for that, I am eternally grateful.

To my **business mentor, Akshar Yadav,** you didn't just teach me marketing; you changed the way I perceive my business and the way I see myself as a business owner.

To my **networking mentor, Mr. Paritosh Pathak,** who opened my eyes to the true power of building genuine relationships with the intention of creating value.

To my **spiritual gurus, Sanjiv Ranjan Ji and Vimal Ji,** your wisdom has been my inner compass, bringing peace and clarity in moments of uncertainty. Your teachings have given me the strength to navigate the unpredictable journey of entrepreneurship.

To my **technology mentors, Prof. Atul Prakash and Suman Saraf,** thank you for sharpening my technical skills and broadening my perspective on innovation and technology. Your guidance has been instrumental in my growth.

To my **friend, Ritika Gupta Dewan,** you understood my vision for this book when it was still taking shape and helped me craft it. Your patience, effort, and attention to detail in proofreading made this book possible.

To my **brother, Nitin Verma,** my co-founder at Orgzit, and the person I turn to for the toughest business decisions – thank you for being my sounding board, and my partner in building Orgzit. This journey wouldn't be the same without you.

To my **wife and business partner, Pooja Verma,** you are my greatest support. You not only help build our business but also manage our family with love and grace, allowing me to give my all to my dreams. Your strength, patience, and belief in me mean everything.

To the joy and light of my life, my **children, Pranit and Pranvi,** your laughter, love, and innocence bring sunshine to my days, reminding me of what truly matters and giving me the motivation to keep pushing forward.

To my **customers,** you have not only placed your trust in me but also entrusted your dreams and goals into my hands. It is a responsibility I hold close to my heart. Every day, you push me, challenge me with your new requests and ideas, and inspire me to think beyond the obvious. Your trust fuels my drive, your challenges expand my vision, and your aspirations make me strive for excellence. I am deeply grateful for this journey we share and for the opportunity to grow alongside you.

To my **GetOverbooked and MNP friends,** thank you for your relentless encouragement, for pushing me to go beyond my limits, and for always reminding me that growth is a journey best taken together.

To my **Team at Orgzit,** you are the heart and soul of what we have built. Without you, Orgzit would be nothing more than an idea on paper. You bring it to life every single day with your dedication, hard work, and belief in our mission. Thank you for standing by me and making this dream a reality.

To **Dinesh Verma and the Pendown Press team,** this book wouldn't exist without your commitment, creativity, and care. Thank you for bringing it to life.

And lastly, to every friend, family member and well-wisher whether named or unnamed, your presence in my life is a blessing.

This journey is bigger than me.

It belongs to all of us.

Thank you from the bottom of my heart.

Why This Book?

1. **Because you're tired of chaos.** This book helps you escape daily confusion caused by poor systems.
2. **Because software shouldn't feel scary.** It breaks things down in a way anyone can understand.
3. **Because your time is valuable.** Learn how to save hours every week with smarter tools.
4. **Because growth needs clarity.** Find the path to organized, efficient, and scalable business operations.
5. **Because you've already tried guessing.** Now it's time to follow a proven roadmap that actually works.

So let's not wait any longer; grab a cup of chai or coffee, whatever you like, and let's begin this journey together.

Introduction

From Struggle to Systems: My Journey to Helping Small Businesses Thrive

When I was in 12th grade, I read *Rich Dad, Poor Dad* for the first time. It felt like reading my own father's story. He was the smartest man I knew – an IIT engineer who ran a small consulting business. He worked tirelessly, sometimes even when his health didn't allow it. He worked over 70 hours a week, yet we were never truly wealthy.

Despite his brilliance and relentless dedication, I saw him struggle, stuck in a cycle of managing day-to-day operations, unable to achieve true financial freedom.

We rarely went on vacations. He was always busy, preoccupied, and mentally consumed by work. As a teenager, I often wondered: *Why does my dad work so hard but still struggle to grow his business? Why can't we afford luxuries like business-class travel or professional tennis coaching for me?*

One day, I came across a quote by Warren Buffett: *"If you do not find a way to make money while you sleep, you will work until you die."*

That hit me hard. It summed up everything I had seen growing up. I realized my father, like so many small business owners, was stuck managing daily operations, with no systems in place to run the business smoothly. The business ran *on them*, not *without them*.

After completing my bachelor's at IIT Delhi and my master's at the University of Michigan, and working in startups and Fortune 500 companies, I started my first software company, but it failed. I had no clue how to manage teams, handle operations, or scale effectively. But in that failure lay the seeds of learning: real, gritty insights that no classroom could have taught me.

Through deep conversations with hundreds of small business owners, I began to see a pattern. Most of them were brilliant at their core work: sales, service, or production but they struggled with building systems. Poor productivity, lack of delegation, and ad hoc decision-making were holding them back. The result was slow growth and stagnation! They were trapped in their own business. I had a burning question: *How can small business owners break free from this cycle?*

That question sparked a lifelong mission in me – to help business owners escape operational chaos and create systems that empower them to thrive, not just survive.

That's when I decided to create Orgzit, a simple yet powerful CRM and ERP system designed to help small business owners organize, automate, and grow without getting stuck in daily tasks.

At Orgzit, we help businesses simplify operations and reduce inefficiencies through business software solutions – so that owners can finally focus on what truly matters: *growth, strategy, and freedom.*

In the last nine years, Orgzit has helped over a hundred businesses streamline their operations, save time, and gain the freedom my father never had. While I couldn't change my father's struggles, helping others like him has become my mission.

And this book is a part of that mission.

Chapter 1

Software Mistakes That Cost $100K+

"A software investment without strategy is just an expensive lesson in failure."

As a business owner, your ultimate goal isn't just to grow, it's to reclaim control over your time, reduce stress, and build a profitable business that operates smoothly without depending entirely on you. A well-implemented software system can be your partner in achieving this.

However, getting it right is no small feat.

As a business software and systems expert, this is one hard truth that I've learned along the way – the success of software implementation doesn't just depend on the solution you select!

Even with the best software solution, the path to a successful software implementation that achieves business objectives is filled with hidden traps. From my experiences, I've learnt that it's critical to avoid the common mistakes that derail most businesses during implementation.

Let the Numbers Speak

Here are some alarming statistics about software investments:

- Approximately 31% of IT projects are deemed complete failures, failing to deliver the expected ROI.
- On average, software projects run over budget by about 45%.
- Software projects typically take 66% longer than initially planned.
- Only 16% of users believe that newly implemented software always meets their needs.

These numbers paint a clear picture: most software projects don't fail due to bad software; they fail due to bad planning.

The Hidden $100K Trap in Software Projects

For many small and midsized businesses, software investments are not just about efficiency – they are critical to survival and growth. Yet, what most business owners don't realize is that when software implementations fail, the real losses go far beyond just the price of the software itself.

A failed software project can easily cost a business $100,000 or more, even for a relatively small implementation. Here's how these costs add up.

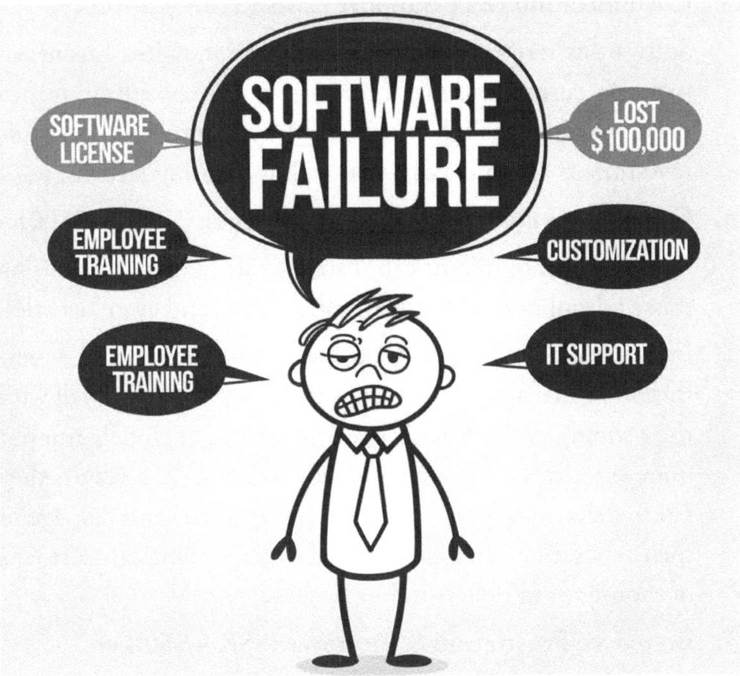

1. **Wasted Software Licensing & Subscription Fees ($10K – $50K+)**

   Many businesses invest in software solutions that they never fully implement or abandon halfway through. Whether it's an expensive CRM or ERP system, an operations management system, or an invoicing tool, subscription fees pile up even when the software isn't delivering value.

2. **Employee Time Lost in Training & Adoption ($10K – $30K)**

   Your team spends weeks, and sometimes months, in learning a system that ultimately doesn't fit their workflow. Every wasted training session and transition period takes away productive hours that could have been used to generate revenue.

3. **Customization & IT Support Costs ($10K – $40K+)**

   Software is rarely a plug-and-play solution. Most businesses invest in customizations, integrations, and consulting fees to make it work for their processes. When a project fails, these investments are sunk costs that will never bring returns.

4. **Operational Disruptions & Lost Revenue ($20K – $100K)**

   A poor software rollout can disrupt daily operations, causing missed deadlines, customer dissatisfaction, and even lost sales.

   Imagine a manufacturing business that implements a new inventory management system that doesn't integrate well with their supply chain. Orders get delayed, raw materials run out unexpectedly, and production slows down. As a result, they fail to deliver on time, leading to lost revenue, and damage to their reputation. The reputational damage alone can cost tens of thousands of dollars in lost business.

5. **Employee Frustration & Turnover ($5K – $50K+)**

   A failed software system doesn't just hurt business efficiency – it affects morale. Employees struggling with broken or inefficient systems lose motivation. Worse, top talent may leave, forcing businesses to spend on recruitment and retraining.

Summary Table: What a Failed Project Could Cost You

Cost Factor	Estimated Loss ($)	Description
Wasted Software Licensing & Subscription Fees	$10K – $50K+	Businesses pay for software they never fully use or abandon halfway, leading to wasted subscription fees.

Employee Time Lost in Training & Adoption	$10K – $30K	Teams spend weeks or months learning a system that doesn't fit, losing valuable work hours.
Customization & IT Support Costs	$10K – $40K+	Customizations, integrations, and IT support add up, and when software fails, these costs are lost.
Operational Disruptions & Lost Revenue	$20K – $100K	Poor software rollout disrupts operations, causing missed deadlines, customer dissatisfaction, and lost sales.
Employee Frustration & Turnover	$5K – $50K+	Frustrated employees lose motivation, and top talent may leave, increasing recruitment and retraining costs.

The Real Cost? More Than Just Money

While $100,000 in direct financial loss is painful, the long-term impact can be even worse. Businesses stuck with inefficient, broken systems find themselves unable to scale, missing out on growth opportunities that could have multiplied their revenue over time.

My objective with this book is to ensure you don't become another software failure statistic. With the right strategy, you can make smarter software decisions, avoid costly mistakes, and turn your software investment into a growth engine, not a liability.

This brings us to the question at the heart of this book.

Why do so many businesses fail at software implementation, and how can you avoid their mistakes?

Here's the truth: **The problem isn't the software!** It's the lack of alignment between the software solution and the actual needs of the business.

Over the years, I've seen too many businesses fall into the same trap – rushing to implement a software system without fully understanding their own goals, processes, and challenges.

They expect the software to magically solve everything, only to find themselves frustrated, stuck, and often worse off than when they started.

Implementing software successfully is all about strategy. You need to make deliberate choices, avoid costly mistakes, and build a system that serves your business, not the other way around.

With the right approach, you can take control, streamline your operations, and create a business that thrives without constant firefighting.

Stop letting inefficiencies and poor decisions hold your business back.

This book is the culmination of my years of experience helping businesses tackle these challenges. I've seen what works and what doesn't. I've learned the hard lessons, and I'm sharing them with you so you don't have to.

My goal is to put as many business owners as possible on the path to freedom – **freedom from endless operations, inefficiencies, and missed opportunities.**

This book is your blueprint for implementing software systems that drive real results. It's time to make smarter choices, build a scalable foundation, and lead your business to sustainable growth.

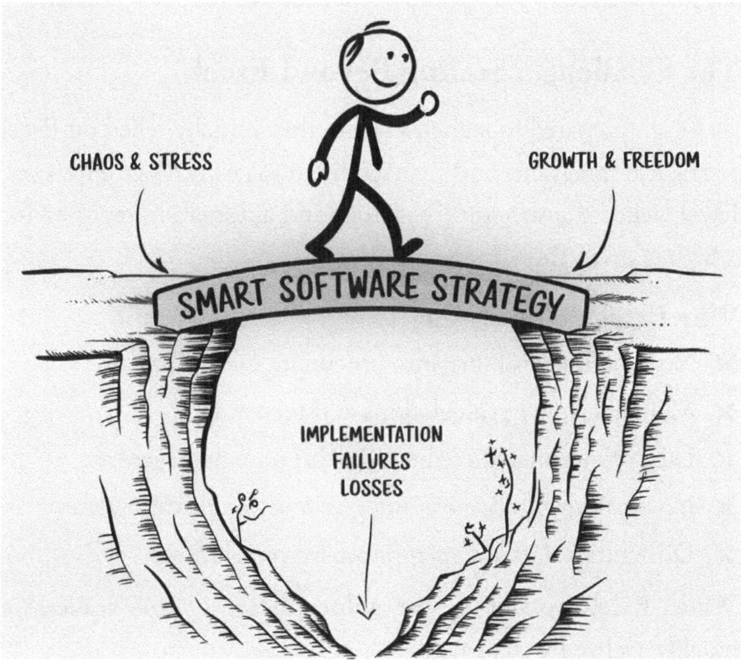

How Origo Commodities Built a Scalable Fintech Business with the Right Software Strategy

Origo Commodities, India's leading agri-tech company, operates across multiple business verticals, including commodity warehousing, procurement finance, and trade facilitation. With a vast network of buyers, sellers, and lenders, Origo had a vision to launch **ProFin**, a procurement finance service designed to help buyers access higher procurement volumes with convenient credit terms while ensuring suppliers received instant payments. The problem? The company was still operating its financial workflows manually in Excel, and this approach could not support the scale, speed, and complexity of this new venture.

The Challenge: Scaling Beyond Excel

As Origo prepared to launch ProFin, they initially relied on Excel to track transactions and manage financial workflows. However, Excel lacked the structure, controls, and automation required for a high-growth fintech operation.

Why Excel Failed Origo

- ✕ No real-time visibility into procurement transactions
- ✕ Manual errors in calculations and reporting
- ✕ Lack of automated credit and debit note management
- ✕ No email or notification integrations for critical updates
- ✕ Difficulties in tracking approvals and cash flows

While Excel worked in the **pilot phase**, Origo's leadership quickly realized a hard truth:

Scaling a financial service without a proper system was a recipe for disaster.

The Wrong Solution: A Failed Custom Software Attempt

Determined to build a scalable tech solution, Origo decided to develop a custom software solution from scratch. The company invested heavily, both time and money, to create a system tailored to ProFin's needs.

What went wrong?

- Over a year of development but **no functional product**
- $40,000 spent on planning, with **nothing usable to show**
- Excessive documentation, **but no tangible results**
- Delays in business launch, leading to **lost opportunities**

The custom software never went live. Despite a detailed requirement document, the project failed due to complexity, continuous delays, and cost overruns. Origo was stuck. They had a promising business model but no **technology to execute it efficiently.**

Mistakes Origo Made

- **Assumed Custom Software Was the Only Option**

  Origo believed that only a fully custom-built system could meet their needs, ignoring faster and more efficient alternatives.

- **Focused on Documentation Instead of Execution**

  Too much time was spent on planning and creating detailed requirement documents, while the actual software remained non-existent.

- **Underestimated the Cost and Complexity of Custom Development**

  Origo assumed that a custom solution would take 6 months – it stretched to over a year with no results.

- **Over-Engineering Crushed Agility**

  Instead of evaluating time-to-market and scalability, Origo focused only on feature requirements, which led to over-engineered complexity.

A New Approach: The Origo – Orgzit Collaboration

After wasting a year on failed software development, Origo's CTO Girish Kathpalia, connected with me. Through focused consulting and in-depth discussions, I recommended a faster, more scalable approach – leveraging **Orgzit's no-code platform** instead of building software from scratch.

- Unlike their previous approach, Orgzit provided a ready-to-use platform that could be customized within weeks, not months.
- **Step 1: Identifying the Core Requirements:** Instead of getting stuck in unnecessary feature lists, Origo focused on the 5 to 6 critical functionalities needed to launch ProFin successfully.
- **Step 2: Rapid Customization**: Using Orgzit's no-code architecture, Origo built a tailored fintech workflow within just three months, achieving results 5X faster than their failed custom software project.
- **Step 3: Testing & Implementation:** The ProFin system was piloted, refined, and fully deployed within a quarter, ensuring a seamless transition from Excel to an automated platform.
- **Step 4: Scaling & Optimization**: With Orgzit's flexibility and ongoing consultation, Origo was able to continuously improve the platform without disrupting operations.

The Results: ProFin Becomes a Scalable Fintech Success

In just three months, ProFin evolved into a scalable Fintech operation. Orgzit's consulting and technology helped Origo transform ProFin from an idea into a fully operational business unit. The impact was immediate:

- **Business Launch & Growth**: ProFin went live 5X faster than originally planned.
- **Revenue Acceleration**: First-year revenue doubled expectations due to seamless operations.
- **Massive Time Savings**: Automated workflows eliminated manual errors and delays.
- **Real-Time Insights**: Executives gained data visibility to make informed business decisions.
- **Scalability Achieved**: ProFin expanded without any additional tech investments.

With Orgzit's no-code technology, Origo **saved over $100,000 in development costs** and scaled its fintech services in just 3 months – instead of the 12+ months it would have otherwise taken.

Key Takeaways

- **Don't assume custom software is the only solution**: Scalable, no-code platforms can deliver results faster and at a fraction of the cost and time.
- **Software implementation should be agile, not over-engineered:** Focus on quick wins and refine the system over time.

Create Your Action Plan

Don't become another $100K mistake. Take these 3 steps now to protect your business from a failed software implementation:

1. **Audit Your Past Software Decisions**

   Reflect on any software you've purchased (or tried to implement) in the last 3 years.

   - *What worked?*
   - *What didn't?*
   - *Did you get the results you expected?*

   Write down one decision that didn't work well and what you'd do differently today.

2. **Calculate Your Hidden Costs**

   Pull up a notepad or Excel sheet and ask yourself:

   Have you silently lost money on the software project?

   - *Subscription fees for unused tools*
   - *Time spent training on the wrong system*
   - *Expensive customizations or consultants that didn't deliver*
   - *Team delays due to tech issues*
   - *Lost deals from missed follow-ups or delays*

   Estimate the total. Even a rough estimate will shock you.

3. **Redesign Your Software Strategy:**

   Think beyond traditional development.

   - Are you prioritizing speed, adaptability, and real results?
   - Could simpler tools or phased rollouts work better than complex builds?
   - Are you testing early instead of planning endlessly?

   The goal is to shift from over-planning to continuous improvement. Build lean, test fast, and stay flexible.

Chapter 2

Software is not a cost, but an investment

> *"Smart businesses think of software as a revenue multiplier, not a line item on the expense sheet."*

Many business owners think twice before spending money on software. They see it as an extra expense – just another bill to pay.

But what if the real cost isn't in the software itself, but in the inefficiencies, lost time, and missed opportunities that come from not using the right tools?

Let's understand the difference between a **cost** and an **investment**.

A **cost** is something you pay for without a direct return, like rent or office supplies.

An **investment**, on the other hand, provides value beyond what you put in, like hiring a great salesperson who multiplies your revenue.

The right software works the same way: it saves time, reduces errors, and helps businesses scale faster with less effort.

The Hidden Cost of "Saving Money" on Software

Business owners who believe that not spending on software saves them money are, in reality, losing more than they realize.

Imagine you run a growing distribution business. Every day, you and your team spend hours tracking orders, following up with customers, managing stock levels, and handling invoices – all manually, using spreadsheets and emails.

At first, it seems manageable. But as your business grows:

- Orders start getting mixed up
- Follow-ups get delayed
- Customers complain about late deliveries
- Payments from customers are delayed
- Your team spends more time fixing mistakes than doing productive work

You might not see it immediately, but these **small inefficiencies cost you real money**. Slowly, they start affecting your profits, reputation, and peace of mind.

Let's see how you are losing money without realizing it.

1. **Wasted Time = Wasted Money**

   Your team's time is valuable. Every minute they spend on manual work is a minute they aren't spending on tasks that actually grow your business.

2. **Mistakes Are Expensive**

   With manual work, errors are inevitable. Wrong invoices, missing stock, double orders – these aren't just small problems. They damage your reputation, cause financial losses, and make customers lose trust in your business.

3. **Mediocre Customer Experience = Lost Customers**

   When customers experience delays, poor service, or miscommunication, they quietly walk away. And in today's competitive world, they won't come back.

   Even losing **a single good customer** due to a poor experience can cost you tens of thousands of dollars in lifetime value. Can you afford that?

4. **Missed Growth Opportunities**

   Without streamlined systems, you're always busy in handling daily operations. You have no time to think about strategic growth initiatives such as expanding offerings, entering new markets, or investing in marketing.

What Happens When You Invest in the Right Software?

1. **You Save Time and Get More Done:** Automation eliminates repetitive tasks, reducing errors and improving efficiency. What once took hours can now be done in minutes.
2. **You Improve Decision-Making:** A software provides real-time data and insights leading to better informed and profitable decisions.
3. **You Scale Without Chaos:** As your business grows, so does complexity. Smart software helps manage that growth in an organized way, ensuring smoother operations and fewer growing pains.
4. **Your Team Collaborates Better:** Employees are more engaged when they spend their time on strategic, creative, and customer-focused work instead of repetitive manual tasks. Good software supports better communication, coordination, and ownership.

A Tale of Two Business Owners: John and Mark

John and Mark both started their businesses with similar dreams – growth, success, and financial freedom. But a couple of years later, their journeys looked completely different.

John's Business – The Struggle Continues

John believed in saving costs, so he continued running his business the old-fashioned way – manually tracking everything using spreadsheets and emails. At first, things seemed under control, but as his business grew, so did his problems:

1. **Missed Orders & Delays:** With no automation, customer follow-ups got delayed, invoices piled up, and orders started getting mixed up.
2. **Frustrated Team:** His employees were unorganized, working without consistent processes.
3. **Unhappy Customers:** Late deliveries and miscommunication led to complaints, cancellations, and lost customers.
4. **Ad hoc Decisions:** Without real data and insights, John couldn't make data-driven decisions, making every decision feel like a gamble.
5. **Reactive not Proactive:** He was always working in a reactive mode putting out immediate fires instead of proactively planning for strategic growth initiatives.

John kept thinking, *"I'm saving money by avoiding expensive software,"* but in reality, his inefficiencies were costing him far more than he realized.

Mark's Business – Scaling with Smart Systems

Mark, on the other hand, saw things differently. Instead of seeing software as an expense, he saw it as an investment in growth. So, he implemented a smart business system that organized his information, implemented business processes and controls, and automated his workflow. The software investment helped him realize the following results:

1. **Effortless Follow-ups:** Automated reminders ensured no customer inquiries were lost, boosting conversion rates.
2. **Smooth Order Processing:** Order status and inventory were visible in real-time, reducing errors and ensuring on-time deliveries.

3. **Happier, More Productive Team:** Employees spent 80% less time on manual tasks, allowing them to focus on sales and higher-value tasks.
4. **Strategy Focus:** Free from day-to-day operations, Mark had the time and energy to focus on strategic business growth initiatives. He used the insights from the software system to identify growth opportunities.

The Big Lesson?

In just a couple of years, Mark's business was thriving, while John's business was still struggling to survive.

The difference between them wasn't luck – it was mindset.

➢ **John focused on cutting costs and saving money. Mark focused on making the right investments to scale smartly.**

- **John saw software as an expense. Mark saw it as a strategic growth tool.**
- **John got stuck in daily operations. Mark built systems to run his day-to-day operations smoothly.**

The million-dollar question is: ***Who do you want to be?***

Growth Thinking: The 3 Big Shifts Business Owners Need to Make

Business owners who have a cost-cutting mindset when it comes to software, end up being stuck in a cycle of low productivity, inefficient processes, spending a lot of time on fixing mistakes – leading to being completely occupied with day-to-day operations.

Successful business owners *think differently.*

They don't ask, *"How much will this cost me?"*

They ask, *"How much will this help me grow?"*

This small shift in thinking changes everything.

If you want to scale your business and not just survive, here are the three mindset shifts you need to make.

1. **From "Expense" to "Return on Investment"**

   ✗ **Wrong Question:** "How much does this software cost?"

   ☑ **Right Question:** "How much time, money, and effort will this software save me in the long run?"

2. **From "Short-Term Cost" to "Long-Term Growth"**

   ✗ **Wrong Question:** "Can I avoid this expense right now?"

   ☑ **Right Question:** "Will this help my business grow consistently over the next 5 years?"

3. From "Manual Effort" to "Scalable Systems"

- ✗ **Wrong Thinking:** "We'll just manage everything manually for now."
- ☑ **Right Thinking:** "I need scalable systems that deliver predictable, consistent results – with or without me being involved 24/7."

The Future Belongs to Businesses That Leverage Technology

- ➢ Businesses that fear spending on systems stay stuck in survival mode.
- ➢ Businesses that invest in the right tools grow faster, operate smarter, and dominate their industries.

Every successful business has one thing in common – **strong systems that reduce manual work, increase efficiency, and free up time to focus on growth.**

If you want to free yourself from daily struggles and focus on real growth, it's time to start thinking differently.

- ➢ Don't just cut costs – invest in your future growth.

How VIP Industries Scaled Its B2B Sales with the Right Software Strategy

VIP Industries, a leader in luggage manufacturing, operates with a highly efficient B2B sales team that sells through multiple institutional channels. The company has built a solid reputation and maintains impressive revenue figures despite having a compact team of just 25 employees. However, despite its strong market presence, VIP faced a significant challenge – it lacked the right digital systems to scale further.

For years, VIP's B2B Sales team managed its sales operations using Excel sheets, tracking opportunities, quotes, follow-ups, and deals manually. While this approach worked to an extent, it severely limited the company's ability to get reports, optimize processes, and unlock new growth opportunities. The absence of structured data meant VIP's team could not:

- Efficiently identify and grow revenue from high-potential customers
- Track sales performance across different geographies and industries
- Gain visibility into missed opportunities and areas for expansion

The Cost of Not Having the Right Systems

Despite being a well-established brand, VIP was unable to scale beyond its existing success. The company had untapped potential, but lacked the ability to measure where and how to grow. Its B2B institutional sales team, while performing well, was stretched to its limits because everything was being managed manually.

Without real-time analytics, VIP had no clear insights into which opportunities and customers had the highest conversion potential, making their sales efforts inefficient.

The Wrong Solution: A Costly Software Misstep

Recognizing the need for a CRM, VIP made what seemed like a safe and logical decision – they chose the biggest and most recognized CRM software in the market: **Salesforce**. The decision was heavily influenced by the company's CIO, who had previously worked with Salesforce in a previous organization, much larger than VIP's B2B Sales division.

Without evaluating whether Salesforce was the right fit for VIP's specific needs, the company invested heavily in its implementation. The project ran for over a year, consuming substantial financial and human resources. However, the outcome was a failure:

- The entire sales team rejected the system
- VIP never fully migrated its sales data
- The software remained unused, despite the time and money spent on it

Salesforce, while a powerful tool, proved to be too complex, expensive, and rigid for VIP's operations. It failed because the team wasn't properly guided through its implementation, and the company lacked a clear strategy for ensuring adoption and long-term usage.

Mistakes VIP Made in Choosing Software

VIP's failure to implement Salesforce successfully was the result of three key mistakes:

1. **Delayed Digital Transformation for Too Long**

   VIP waited too long. By treating software as a cost rather than an investment, they lost years of potential growth. Had they adopted the right tools earlier, they could have scaled faster, with fewer growing pains.

2. **Chose a Brand Name Over Business Fit**

   Rather than choosing a system based on their unique needs, VIP chose the biggest brand. The assumption that "bigger is better" led to a misaligned implementation.

3. **Ignored Change Management & Team Adoption**

   The team was never brought into the process. There was no structured onboarding or adoption strategy, which made rejection inevitable.

A New Approach: Finding the Right Partner for Success

After the failure of Salesforce, VIP re-evaluated its strategy and sought a solution that was:

- ➢ Customizable to their B2B sales process
- ➢ Easy to implement without disrupting operations
- ➢ Adoptable by their sales team without resistance

This led them to Orgzit – a CRM & workflow automation platform for B2B businesses. Unlike Salesforce, Orgzit was designed to be lightweight, intuitive, and flexible, aligning perfectly with VIP's needs.

But this time, the *implementation approach* made all the difference:

What VIP Did Differently This Time

Instead of repeating past mistakes, VIP worked with us and took a different approach, one that helped them avoid past mistakes. This led to:

- ➢ **Step 1: Understanding the Sales Process**: Orgzit's team conducted a deep dive into VIP's sales operations to identify gaps and inefficiencies.
- ➢ **Step 2: Pilot Testing**: A customized sales tracking system was implemented in a controlled environment for six months to ensure usability.

- **Step 3: Gradual Rollout**: Rather than an overnight switch, Orgzit was introduced module by module, allowing the team to adapt smoothly.
- **Step 4: Dedicated Support & Coaching**: Unlike before, VIP received continuous handholding and training, ensuring 100% adoption and usage across the team.

The Results: A Scalable, Growth-Ready System

Within a year of implementing Orgzit, VIP achieved remarkable improvements:

- Real-time visibility into sales performance
- Ability to break down and analyze sales performance by various parameters
- Higher lead conversions with structured follow-ups
- Time saved by eliminating Excel-based tracking
- Data-driven decision-making for better sales strategies

Most importantly, they future-proofed their business, setting up a scalable system to power 5X growth over the next decade.

Key Takeaways

Here are the key takeaways from VIP's journey to transform their sales operations:

- Choosing the **right-fit system** is more important than choosing the biggest name.
- A **step-by-step, agile approach** leads to higher adoption and better results.
- **Implementation and support** matter just as much as the software selection.

- Having an **expert as a partner** makes all the difference by ensuring the right strategy and execution.

The right software isn't an expense – it's the foundation for your scalable success.

Create Your Action Plan

After reading this chapter, take a moment to reflect on how you view software in your business. Answer these two questions to start shifting from a **cost mindset** to a **growth mindset**:

1. **Identify Your Hidden Costs:** What daily manual tasks or inefficiencies are costing you time and money?

   List three areas where being better organized or having automation could save time and reduce errors.

2. **Define Your Growth Goals:** Identify one area of your business where a system could improve efficiency, reduce stress, and increase revenue, and commit to exploring a software solution for it.

Chapter 3

The First Step Most Businesses Neglect

> ***"Buying software without clear objectives is like setting sail without a map – you'll drift, not arrive."***

When it comes to implementing new software, the most common pitfall is not defining clear business objectives. Often, in the rush to jump onto a trend or follow a recommendation, we overlook the foundational step of aligning our goals with the software we're investing in.

Imagine this: You attend a networking event or a business party, and someone mentions a software they're using with great success. Inspired, you rush to your team the next day and instruct them to look into it for immediate implementation. But just because something worked well for another company doesn't mean it's the right fit for yours. Decisions made on hearsay, without proper evaluation, often lead to wasted resources and regrettable outcomes.

Here's what you need to keep in mind to avoid this trap and ensure your software serves its intended purpose effectively:

1. **Start with Real Insights and Experience**

   Before making any decisions, take a moment to reflect on the real needs of your business. What specific challenges are you facing? This judgment should come from your real insights and experience rather than impulse or external influence. Recognize the problems you aim to solve and base your objectives on your unique business landscape.

2. **Validate Objectives with Key Stakeholders**

   Imagine a mid-sized manufacturing company implementing a new ERP system to streamline its operations. The management team sets a primary goal of reducing inventory holding costs by 20%. Excited by the potential cost savings, they move forward without consulting other key stakeholders.

   A few months into the implementation, the production team starts facing delays. Why? The system doesn't account for the specific scheduling requirements of their just-in-time production process. Meanwhile, the sales team struggles with entering custom order details because the ERP's interface wasn't designed to handle complex sales contracts. These overlooked details lead to frustrated employees, delayed deliveries, and a rise in customer complaints.

Now, let's rewind and consider what could have been done differently. Before finalizing the objectives, the company organizes stakeholder workshops, inviting representatives from production, sales, inventory management, and customer service. Through these discussions:

- ➢ The production team highlights the need for real-time scheduling tools.
- ➢ The sales team emphasizes the importance of a customizable order entry feature.
- ➢ The customer service team stresses the need for seamless integration with the CRM.

With these insights, the management team adjusts the objectives, ensuring the ERP system aligns with the operational realities of every department. When the system is eventually implemented, all teams will be better equipped to use it effectively, and the company achieves its goals with minimal disruption.

3. **Document Your Objectives in a One-Page Strategy**

   Avoid overly complicated documentation. Instead, create a clear, concise, one-page strategy that outlines:

- ➢ **The Problem**: What are the core issues you want the software to solve?
- ➢ **Expected Benefits**: What results are you expecting in your business?
- ➢ **Functionality Expectations**: How do you expect the software to work on a day-to-day basis to achieve the results?
- ➢ **User Roles**: Who will be using this software, and how often?

This one-page document serves as your compass, bringing clarity to all stakeholders and establishing a realistic framework for what the software should achieve.

4. **Assign a Responsible Driver to Avoid Indecision by Committee**

   While many people may contribute ideas, only one person should drive the decision-making and implementation process. This **main driver** will coordinate feedback, secure buy-in from key stakeholders, and ensure the alignment of objectives across departments. They serve as the project's anchor, preventing it from becoming a case of "too many cooks spoiling the broth."

Decisions made by committees can often lead to confusion, diluted priorities, and complications. Empowering a single person to take responsibility ensures that all feedback and concerns are filtered through a cohesive vision. This approach keeps the process streamlined, avoids delays, and maintains focus on the core objectives.

Clear objectives are the foundation of a successful software implementation. When everyone is aligned and knows what they're working towards, the chances of success increase significantly. By designating a responsible leader to **document**, **validate**, and **drive** objectives, you save time, resources, and unnecessary headaches in the long run.

Create Your Action Plan

Before implementing new software, take a step back and ensure you have clarity on your objectives. Answer these questions to create your own action plan:

1. **What are the top three challenges in your business that the software solution could help solve?** *(Example: Slow response time to customers, inaccurate inventory tracking, or difficulty managing leads.)*
2. **Who will be the key users of this software, and what specific features do they need to make their work easier?** *(Example: Sales team needs automated follow-ups, finance team needs real-time invoicing and automated collection follow-ups, operations team needs better order tracking.)*

Take five minutes to write your answers. This simple exercise will ensure you make a well-informed decision and choose a software that truly supports your business growth.

Chapter 4

Know Your Success to Achieve It

"Without a scoreboard, you won't know if you're winning or losing."

When it comes to implementing new software in a business, we often focus on the features, functionalities, and deployment timelines. However, one of the most critical steps that can often be overlooked is defining **clear success criteria**. Without a clear benchmark, it's impossible to gauge the impact of the software or understand if it's truly meeting business objectives. This chapter will explore why having measurable, objective success criteria is essential for the success of any software implementation.

Why Success Criteria Matter

The benefits of a new software system can vary widely, from increasing revenue and reducing costs to improving productivity and streamlining workflows. But these benefits are only meaningful if they're tied to specific, measurable criteria that every stakeholder agrees upon.

Clear success criteria provide direction and purpose, ensuring all stakeholders, from management to end-users, are aligned on what they're working toward. It's like setting a North Star for the project, a guiding light that helps everyone stay on track and focused on the end goal. When everyone knows the criteria for success, it becomes easier to track progress, make adjustments, and ultimately, evaluate whether the software is delivering value.

Examples of Success Metrics

When setting success criteria, think clearly about what the software is intended to achieve. Some common benefits of software implementation include:

1. **Revenue Growth**: Does the software contribute to new sales opportunities, higher customer retention, or overall revenue increase?

2. **Cost Reduction:** Can the software help reduce operational costs by streamlining internal processes, improving accuracy, or minimizing manual errors?
3. **Productivity Boost:** Is the software enabling faster task completion or reducing time spent on repetitive tasks?

Defining these metrics as part of your success criteria helps transform the software project from a tech upgrade into a business growth enabler. With these tangible goals in place, your team has a clear target – and your investment has a clear purpose.

Objective Success Criteria: A Shared Vision

Defining success criteria shouldn't happen in isolation. It's essential to involve all stakeholders – from management to end-users – to ensure that everyone's expectations are aligned and realistic.

Equally important is sharing these success criteria with your software partner. They need to understand exactly what success looks like for your organization – **not just from a technical standpoint, but from a business impact perspective**.

When stakeholders agree on the success criteria from the beginning, it creates a unified vision for the project. This shared vision helps avoid misunderstandings and ensures that everyone is working toward the same outcome.

It also gives you a roadmap to hold the software provider accountable and ensure they're delivering a solution that meets your specific needs.

Cause-Effect Relationship

An essential part of setting success criteria is understanding the cause-effect relationship. It's crucial to identify which actions, features, or processes will directly contribute to achieving each defined goal.

For instance, if a CRM system is expected to increase sales, you should clearly define which aspects of the software (e.g., improved lead tracking, and automated follow-ups) will drive this outcome.

This clarity helps connect efforts to results, making the software's contribution easier to track and justify.

Keeping Success Criteria Easy to Measure

The success criteria should be straightforward and easy to measure. Ambiguous or overly complex metrics can lead to confusion and make it difficult to evaluate the effectiveness of the software.

For example, instead of setting a vague goal like "increase productivity," a more specific criteria could be "**reduce the time spent on data entry by 30% within six months of implementation.**" This clarity makes it easier to measure progress objectively and assess the software's impact.

Limit Success Criteria to What Truly Matters

While defining success criteria is crucial, having too many can dilute focus and lead to confusion. Instead of creating a long list of objectives, prioritize the top **two or three most impactful criteria** that directly align with your project's goals. This sharp focus ensures clarity and keeps all stakeholders working toward the same key outcomes.

For smaller projects, **one or two well-defined success criteria** might suffice, while larger projects can have up to three – but no more. Limiting your criteria doesn't mean limiting your vision; it means sharpening it. Fewer, well-thought-out criteria help maintain momentum and ensure that every effort contributes to **achieving tangible, trackable results**.

Examples of Success Criteria

1. **Revenue Growth:** Increase monthly recurring revenue by 15% within the first year of implementation.
2. **Operational Efficiency:** Reduce average time spent on manual data entry by 30% within three months.
3. **Error Reduction:** Minimize invoicing errors by 50% within the first quarter.
4. **Customer Satisfaction:** Improve customer satisfaction scores (CSAT) by 10% within six months.
5. **Task Automation:** Automate 40% of repetitive tasks to save an average of 8 hours per salesperson every week.

Tip: Choose examples that are realistic and directly connected to your software's purpose.

Create Your Action Plan

Before implementing a new software system, take a step back and define what success looks like for your business. Getting this clarity early on will guide every phase of your project. Answer these two questions to ensure your software delivers measurable results:

1. **What are the top three success criteria that will indicate your software implementation is successful?** *(Example: Reduce manual data entry by 30%, increase customer retention by 10%, or automate follow-ups to improve sales efficiency.)*

2. **How will you measure these success criteria, and what timeframe will you set for achieving them?** *(Example: Track time spent on data entry before and after implementation over a three-month period.)*

Write down your answers and use them as a guide throughout the software implementation process. When success is clearly defined and consistently measured, achieving it becomes much easier.

Chapter 5

The Checklist Myth

"A checklist can tell you what a software has, but only strategy can tell you if it's the right fit."

Imagine you're about to purchase a new car. You're handed a long checklist with all sorts of features listed – engine power, AC, power steering, airbags, cup holders. But there's a problem. Buying either a budget hatchback or a luxury sedan may meet basic needs, but the cost, experience, and value they offer are worlds apart.

So, focusing solely on a checklist may mislead you into thinking that two cars, or in our case, two software solutions, are equal – when they're not.

This is the danger of the "Checklist Approach" in evaluating software.

The Problem with the Checklist Approach

Most businesses create a requirements list for their software needs and then match it against a software provider's feature list. On the surface, it seems logical. But here's why it doesn't work:

1. **Fails to Capture True Business Needs:** Instead of a generic checklist, what's often needed are high-level requirements that are subjective and focused on real business impact. A

checklist might include 50 features, but only 3 to 5 of those are truly essential for meeting your company's goals.

2. **All Features are Given Equal Weight:** In a checklist, every item has the same importance. There's no distinction between what's critical for your business and what's nice to have. It ignores the 80-20 rule – where 20% of the features provide 80% of the value.
3. **Easily Manipulated by Vendors:** Checklists can be misleading. A vendor might appear to meet all requirements simply by ticking off boxes, but that doesn't mean their software aligns with your business's core objectives. Just like how both an entry-level car and a luxury car meet basic checklist criteria but serve very different experiences.

A Better Approach – Criteria that Aligns with Business Objectives

Instead of relying on a long checklist, here's how to make your software evaluation more effective:

1. **Define Key Objectives:** Start by identifying the top 3 to 5 objectives that are most crucial for your business. These should be high-level goals that directly align with your business strategy, not a laundry list of features.
2. **Prioritize Based on Business Impact:** Assign weightage to each objective based on how much value it drives. Recognize that certain capabilities will have a much bigger impact on your business than others. This way, you avoid getting lost in the details and stay focused on what truly matters.
3. **Stay Subjective Where It Matters:** While it's tempting to create a feature-by-feature comparison, it's often more helpful to stay subjective and evaluate whether the software meets

your needs in practical, impactful ways. Does it fit your company culture, your workflows, and your long-term goals? Often, a subjective but practical evaluation reveals more than a checklist ever can.

Create Your Action Plan

Take a step back and evaluate beyond the checklist. Answer these questions to ensure you're choosing the right solution for your business needs:

1. **What are the top 3-5 business objectives that this software must help you achieve?**

   (Think beyond features – focus on outcomes like increasing efficiency, improving customer experience, or automating key workflows.)

2. **What software capabilities are truly essential to achieving these objectives?**

   (Prioritize based on business impact. Don't get distracted by "nice to have" features that add complexity but no real value.)

Chapter 6

If They Don't Use It, It Won't Work

"The best software isn't the one with the most features – it's the one people actually use."

When it comes to implementing new software systems, one of the most common mistakes businesses make is overlooking the needs of the end users. Often, management selects software based solely on high-level requirements and strategic objectives, without consulting the team members who will actually use the system day-to-day. This oversight can lead to a range of issues, from low adoption rates and constant workarounds to outright resistance from the people who need the software the most.

Why Ignoring the End User Is a Big Mistake

Imagine you're redesigning your home. You hire an architect, discuss grand designs, and finalize the layout, all without consulting the family members who will actually live in the house. Once it's built, you realize the kitchen is too small for daily cooking, the kids' study room doesn't have enough lighting, and the bedroom layout doesn't suit anyone's preferences.

The house might look great on paper, but it fails to serve the people who need it the most.

This is exactly what happens when management selects a software system without involving the end users. The result is a system that looks good but doesn't fit the day-to-day needs of those who will rely on it, leading to frustration, low adoption rates, and ultimately the software failing to meet business objectives.

Here are some reasons why ignoring the end user can lead to problems:

1. **Feeling Left Out**: When end users aren't part of the selection process, they often feel ignored and left out. They may think that the new software isn't meant to make their jobs easier but rather just to satisfy the management's objectives. This lack of engagement can quickly lead to frustration, resistance, and a lack of ownership over the new system.
2. **Choosing the Wrong Software**: Without feedback from those who will actually use the software, businesses risk selecting a solution that doesn't fit their needs. The software may end up being too complicated, difficult to navigate, or simply inefficient for the tasks it was intended to handle.
3. **Increased Complexity and Training Needs**: A system chosen without considering the end user can end up being overly complex. If the software is hard to use, the employees will avoid it or use it incorrectly. This not only defeats the purpose of implementing the software but also results in wasted time, money, and effort on training sessions that could have been avoided with the right system.

How to Ensure End Users Are Part of the Process

To avoid these pitfalls, it's crucial to involve end users in both the software selection and implementation process. Here's how:

1. **Engage Early and Listen**: Before making any decisions, invite end users to participate in discussions about the new system. Ask them what they need, what challenges they currently face, and how they think the software could help them. Their insights are invaluable and often highlight practical needs that decision-makers might overlook.

2. **Demo and Trial Phases**: Allow end users to test the software through demos and trial phases. Let them get hands-on experience with the system and provide feedback on its usability, complexity, and effectiveness. This helps ensure that the chosen software aligns with their needs.
3. **Select User-Friendly Software**: Opt for software solutions that are simple, intuitive, and easy to navigate. Complicated software is unlikely to be fully adopted, especially if it doesn't make the end user's work easier or more efficient. Prioritize usability over flashy features that might look good on paper but don't add value to daily operations.

Create Your Action Plan

Ensuring end-user adoption is critical to the success of any software implementation. Use these questions to assess whether you're making the right choices for your team:

1. **Have you involved the actual users in the decision-making process?**

   (Gather their feedback early. Identify their pain points and ensure the software solves real, everyday challenges for them.)
2. **Is the software intuitive and easy to use, or will it require extensive training?**

   (If the system is too complex, adoption rates will drop. Prioritize usability over unnecessary features.)

Chapter 7

Why Bigger Isn't Always Better

> ***"The right partner isn't the one who's the biggest – it's the one who cares the most."***

A few years ago, a close friend of mine was growing her business and decided it was time to implement a Customer Relationship Management (CRM) system. She wanted to make her work easier and prepare for future growth. Like many others, she chose a big, well-known software company because of its reputation.

At first, the CRM promised to save her time, improve customer relationships, and give useful insights for growing the business. But soon, things didn't go as planned.

Whenever she needed help, she had to call customer support and was passed from one department to another. The calls took forever, and the answers felt scripted. Every time, she was told, "Your issue has been escalated," but nothing ever got fixed. The lack of accountability made her feel like just another ticket in the system.

Weeks turned into months, and instead of making things better, the CRM created more frustration. What was supposed to be a solution had now become a bottleneck.

On top of that, when she wanted to add more functionality, the software provider informed her that she would need to upgrade to a higher-tier plan. This plan included several features her business didn't require, but the company's rigid pricing structure left her with no other option.

Instead of tailoring the software to her needs, the software organization seemed more focused on upselling their premium plans.

Her team was still stuck doing things manually, and the software that was supposed to help her just added to her problems.

The rigid processes and lack of flexibility from the provider made it clear that their solution was not built to cater to the unique and evolving needs of a growing business like hers.

A big lesson here – Bigger isn't always better when it comes to choosing a software partner. What matters more is how much they understand you, support you, and grow with you.

The Challenges of Working with Large Vendors

My friend's experience wasn't one-off; it's a typical challenge many small businesses face when working with large software providers. While large organizations bring strengths like robust systems, global reach, and vast resources, these very strengths can become barriers when dealing with the specific and evolving needs of a small business.

Here are some common challenges small businesses encounter with large vendors:

1. **Lack of Personalization:** Large vendors operate on standardized processes designed to cater to a broad customer base. While this works for large businesses, it leaves smaller businesses struggling to fit into rigid workflows that don't align with their operations.
2. **Slow Issue Resolution:** With multiple layers of support, issues are often passed between teams, leading to delayed resolutions. Small businesses, which rely on quick fixes to maintain operations, often feel sidelined.
3. **Minimal Accountability:** Large organizations often lack a dedicated point of contact. This can leave smaller clients feeling like just another number in a long queue.
4. **Rigid Pricing Structures:** Large companies typically offer tiered pricing with limited flexibility. Businesses are forced to upgrade to higher tiers for some additional features, even if they don't need the entire new plan. This "all-or-nothing" pricing model can leave small businesses overpaying for features they don't use.

The Advantages of Working with Boutique Software Providers

In contrast, boutique software providers bring a different energy and a more human approach. Their agility, personalized service, and commitment to understanding your business make them invaluable partners for small businesses.

Here's why smaller boutique providers might be the better choice:

1. **Personalized Service:** Boutique vendors prioritize building relationships with their clients. Instead of a faceless support team, you often get a dedicated point of contact who deeply understands your business and goals.

2. **Flexibility and Adaptability:** Unlike large vendors bound by bureaucratic approval processes, boutique providers can quickly adapt their solutions to meet your specific needs. For example, they might customize features or workflows to better align with your operations.
3. **Accountability:** In boutique firms, ownership is clear and personal. They're invested in your success, and when things go wrong, they respond faster, fix more thoroughly, and often go the extra mile because every client truly matters.

How Smart Sales & Quoting Systems Powered CAVH's Rise to Florida's Top 3 HVAC Companies

CAVH, one of Florida's leading HVAC solutions providers, had built a strong reputation in the industry. However, as the company grew, its manual sales and quoting processes became major bottlenecks.

Like many businesses, CAVH relied on Excel and manual workflows to manage its sales and quoting process. While this worked initially, it soon became a liability. CAVH began to struggle with:

1. **Errors & Inconsistencies:** Manual spreadsheets caused calculation errors, leading to frequent misquotes
2. **Sluggish Approvals:** Lengthy approval cycles resulted in delays and missed deals
3. **Lack of Real-Time Sales Data:** Without visibility into sales performance, growth strategies were unclear
4. **Lack of Collaboration:** Sales, Estimation, and Operations teams worked in silos, leading to miscommunication and operational inefficiencies

5. **Lack of Consistent Processes:** The absence of a consistent system made it hard to deliver a predictable customer experience

For Carolyn Arote, President of CAVH, these inefficiencies meant lost opportunities and limited scalability. She knew her business had immense potential, but without the right systems, she couldn't unlock it.

The Turning Point: Carolyn's Vision & the Right Partner

Rather than settling for a one-size-fits-all software, Carolyn took charge and set forth to build a system that worked for her business. She knew exactly what CAVH needed and wanted a solution that fit, not one that forced her team to change the way they worked.

That's when she partnered with Orgzit to build the right system for CAVH.

Carolyn brought her deep understanding of CAVH's business, while we helped her translate her ideas into a fully functional software system.

Every feature, every automation, and every workflow was customized to match how CAVH operated. With Orgzit's no-code platform and expert consulting, Carolyn wasn't just getting a tool, she was shaping a system that was her own.

Together, we implemented:

- **A Centralized Sales Dashboard:** Everything from sales to quotes to approvals in one place
- **Automated Approvals:** No more manual back-and-forth, leading to faster deal closures

- **Real-Time Reports:** Sales performance analysis was available instantly, helping to make faster and better decisions
- **Better Team Collaboration:** Estimators, sales, operations, and accounts teams worked seamlessly together, boosting efficiency
- **Automated Reminders:** Ensure that no task, no deadline, and no follow-up is ever missed

By building a system around her vision, Carolyn turned slow, manual processes and disconnected teams into a well-oiled, scalable operation – one that could support CAVH's growth without bottlenecks.

The Results: A Faster, Smarter, More Scalable CAVH

- **Higher quote output per estimator:** More quotes sent meant more deals closed
- **Easier team management:** Streamlined training and performance evaluation of team members
- **Well-defined system for scaling:** With proper systems in place across every core function, CAVH is now able to focus on growth

By leveraging Orgzit's expertise, CAVH quickly grew to become **Florida's No. 3 HVAC** business and is now scaling faster than ever.

"Orgzit has been a game-changer for CAVH! With its familiar Excel-like interface, our team adapted quickly, and the centralized dashboard gave us real-time visibility into projects and tasks. Tracking job schedules is effortless, and the team is able to see in real-time what needs to get done. Seamless communication across teams has enhanced collaboration and accountability. Having a centralized system has helped us implement training, reduce errors, and ensure consistency. Orgzit is worth its weight in gold!"

– Carolyn Arote
President, CAVH HVAC

The Key Takeaway

For small businesses, the choice of software partner can make a world of difference. While big names may seem like a safe bet, their rigid structures and lack of personalization often lead to frustration. Smaller boutique providers, with their agility and focus on customer success, are better positioned to provide the support and solutions that align with your goals.

When selecting a software partner, ask yourself:

- Do they understand my business' unique challenges?
- Are they flexible enough to adapt to my needs?
- Can they provide the personalized attention my business requires?

Sometimes, the best partner is not the one with the biggest brand but the one who is most genuinely committed to your success.

Create Your Action Plan

Choosing the right software vendor can make or break your business operations. Answer these questions to guide your decision:

1. **Is your software partner aligned with your business needs, or are they forcing you into rigid workflows and pricing plans?**

   (Ensure the vendor is willing to adapt to your requirements rather than making you adjust to their system.)

2. **Are you getting personalized support and quick issue resolution, or are you stuck in endless customer support loops?**

(A responsive and accountable partner will save you time, frustration, and hidden costs.)

Chapter 8

Think ROI, Not Just Price

"A low price may look smart today, but only ROI proves wisdom tomorrow."

Many business owners, especially those running small and mid-sized businesses, make the mistake of choosing software based mostly on price. They look for low-cost options, thinking they are saving money. But, in reality, focusing only on price costs far more in the long run.

Imagine the owner of a delivery business is buying a vehicle for his business. He finds a really cheap one and thinks, "Great! I saved money." But soon, he realizes that it breaks down often, requires expensive repairs, and slows down deliveries. Instead of saving money, he loses time, customers, and revenue. The same logic applies to business software.

The real question when choosing software shouldn't be "How much does it cost?" but rather, "How much will it help my business grow and operate more efficiently?"

This is where Return on Investment (ROI) comes in. The right software is not an expense; it's an investment that saves time, increases efficiency, and boosts profits. In this chapter, we'll explore why focusing on ROI, and not just the price tag, is the smarter way to choose software.

Why ROI Should Be Your Focus – Not Just the Price Tag

Smart business owners don't ask, "What's the cheapest software I can buy?" Instead, they ask, "What software will give me the best return on my investment?"

ROI (Return on Investment) measures how much value an investment brings compared to its cost.

A higher price tag doesn't mean a bad deal – it often means better efficiency, fewer errors, and more revenue in the long run.

Instead of using price as the primary buying criterion, evaluate the software solution based on its ROI. Ask yourself:

- Will this solution help me set up scalable systems?
- Can it improve my team's productivity and reduce operational inefficiencies?
- How will it contribute to long-term business growth?

Let's look at John, who runs a distribution business. He needs a CRM (Customer Relationship Management) system to track his sales pipeline and manage follow-ups. He considers two options:

- **Option A**: A cheap CRM that costs $50/month, but it lacks automated follow-ups, reporting, and integration with email, causing sales reps to manually update records and miss key opportunities.
- **Option B**: A more expensive CRM that costs $200/month, that automates follow-ups, provides real-time reports, and improves the sales team's productivity.

John picks the cheaper option to save money. Six months later, his sales team misses out on multiple deals due to poor follow-ups, costing him $15,000 in lost revenue.

The lesson: Cheap software often turns out to be the costliest mistake.

If a solution saves time, boosts sales, and improves efficiency, it's an investment, not an **expense**.

The Two Types of Costs in Software Implementation

In software implementation, costs resemble an iceberg – what's visible above the surface is much smaller than what lies hidden beneath. While buying and implementing software solutions, ***external costs*** **are easier to see**, but they are just a fraction of the *internal costs* that remain largely unseen yet have a greater long-term impact.

1. **External Costs:** These are the costs you pay directly to the software provider or implementation partner. They typically include:
   - Software license or subscription fees
   - Implementation and setup fees
   - Training and onboarding fees
   - Support and maintenance fees
   - Customization and integration fees
   - Upgrade or enhancement charges over time

   While external costs are visible and easy to calculate, they are only a small fraction of the total investment in a successful software implementation.
2. **Internal Costs:** These are the hidden costs – the bulk of the iceberg below the surface that often go unnoticed but can make or break your ROI. Internal costs include:
   - **Team time spent for training & onboarding:** The hours and productivity lost while your team learns the new system.
   - **User Experience & Usability:** If the software is complex or unintuitive, your team may struggle to adapt and tasks might take longer, wasting valuable time.
   - **Support Needs:** Frequent troubleshooting or a lack of proper support can slow down operations.
   - **Future Enhancements:** The ongoing cost of customizing, modifying, or scaling the software to meet your growing business needs.

External costs are the tip of the iceberg – they are visible and seem like a major cost, but in fact are only a small fraction of the total cost.

Internal costs, though harder to quantify, often outweigh external costs. Ignoring these can lead to significant inefficiencies and missed opportunities.

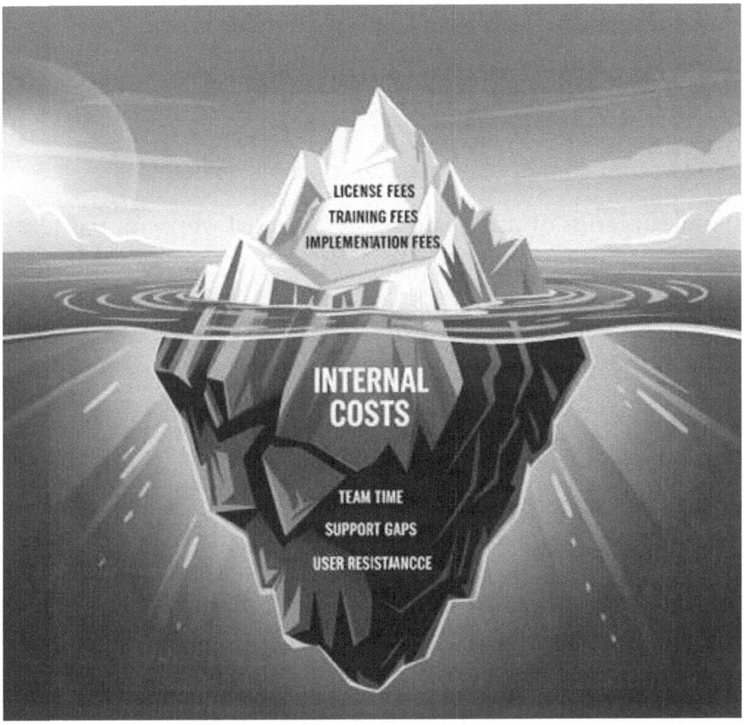

How to Calculate ROI on Business Software

Many business owners hesitate to invest in software because they only see the cost upfront – not the savings, revenue gains, and business growth the software will create over time. But smart business owners know that the right software pays for itself many times over.

Here's a simple 3-step formula to calculate ROI before making a decision:

Step 1: Identify the Key Benefits

Ask yourself:

- What problems will this software solve?
- How much time will it save?
- How much more revenue can it help generate?

Think in terms of daily pain points, manual work, missed leads, poor follow-ups, or inefficiencies and imagine the ease and speed once they're solved.

Step 2: Assign a financial value to the benefits

For example, consider Paul, who runs a consulting business with a team of 20 members. He is considering a CRM system to manage client interactions.

- Paul's team spends 10 hours per week tracking leads manually.
- **His team's average hourly rate is $20 per hour → That means $200 in team cost per week spent on tracking leads.**
- Paul is considering a CRM that automates lead tracking and can cut manual work by 80%, saving $160 per week.

Step 3: Compare the Cost vs. the Benefit

- **CRM Cost:** $200 per month
- **Total Savings:** $640 per month ($160 per week x 4 weeks)
- **Net Gain:** $640 - $200 = $440 in every month
- **ROI:** $440/$200 x 100 = 220%

Every month, the CRM pays for itself multiple times over.

The formula for computing ROI is

$$ROI = \frac{Gain\ from\ Investment - Cost\ of\ Investment}{Cost\ of\ Investment} \times 100$$

The Smarter Way to Think About Software Costs

Don't just ask, *"Is this worth buying?"* Ask, *"What's the hidden price of doing nothing?"*

- ➢ Manual work and cheap software cost more in the long run.
- ➢ Smart software that improves efficiency is an investment that pays for itself many times over.

Business owners who focus on **ROI over price** make better software decisions, save more money, and grow faster with confidence.

How to Calculate ROI: A Real-Life Walkthrough

"The numbers never lie. When in doubt, let ROI do the talking."

To truly understand the ROI (Return on Investment) of software, let us walk you through a real example featuring Peter, the owner of a real estate agency with a small sales team. We'll break down how much time and money his team spends on manual work, and what changes when they implement a CRM system.

This method can be used by any business to calculate the ROI of their own software investments.

➢ **Step 1: Define Your Team Structure**

Start by listing the key roles in your team. In Peter's case, the team includes:

- 10 Sales Executives
- 2 Sales Managers
- 1 Business Owner (Peter himself)

These three roles will form the basis of the calculation.

➢ **Step 2: List the Key Activities for Each Role**

Next, identify the repetitive manual tasks that each role regularly performs, especially those that could be streamlined or automated using a CRM. For example:

- **Sales Executives**:
    - Logging new leads
    - Following up and updating lead status
    - Scoring and qualifying leads
    - Sharing project information with prospects
    - Scheduling meetings or site visits
    - Matching leads with available inventory

- **Sales Managers**:
  - Reviewing sales updates from the team
- **Business Owner**:
  - Monitoring and reviewing the overall sales pipeline

These are the routine activities that consume time every week.

➢ **Step 3: Estimate the Frequency of Each Activity**

Now, for each activity, estimate how often it's performed by one person in a week.

For example, a sales executive might do the following activities:

- Log 10 new leads/week
- Do 20 follow-ups/week
- Schedule 10 meetings/week

Repeat this step for each activity and role to get a complete picture.

Then, multiply the weekly frequency by 4 to estimate the monthly activity volume.

Role	Activity	Frequency per week
Sales Executive	Logging new leads	10
Sales Executive	Following up with leads & updating status	20
Sales Executive	Lead scoring & qualification	10
Sales Executive	Share project details over email or WhatsApp	10

Sales Executive	Meeting & Site Visit Scheduling	10
Sales Executive	Inventory Matching with Leads	10
Sales Manager	Review team sales updates	5
Business Owner	Review overall sales pipeline	1

➢ **Step 4: Record Time Spent – With & Without CRM**

Next, estimate how much time (in minutes) one instance of each activity takes **without CRM** (manual tools like Excel or Google Sheets), and how much time it would take **with a CRM**.

For instance:

- Logging a lead might take **5 minutes manually**, but only **2 minutes with CRM** with automated lead capturing.
- Sharing project info might take 10 minutes manually, but only 2 minutes with automation.

You do this for all activities across all roles.

Role	Activity	Time spent without CRM (minutes)	Time spent with CRM (minutes)
Sales Executive	Logging new leads	5	2
Sales Executive	Following up with leads & updating status	5	2

Sales Executive	Lead scoring & qualification	5	2
Sales Executive	Share project details over email or WhatsApp	10	2
Sales Executive	Meeting & Site Visit Scheduling	5	2
Sales Executive	Inventory Matching with Leads	10	5
Sales Manager	Review sales updates	30	10
Business Owner	Review overall sales pipeline	30	10

➢ **Step 5: Calculate Monthly Time Spent Per Activity**

Now that you have:

- The number of times each activity is done per month
- The time taken per instance – with and without CRM

You can calculate the **total monthly hours** spent per activity.

Example:

- 10 logs/week × 4 weeks = 40 logs/month
- 40 logs × 5 minutes = 200 minutes manually = 3.3 hours/month
- 40 logs × 2 minutes = 80 minutes with CRM = 1.3 hours/month
- **Time saved = 2 hours/month per person**

Repeat this for every activity and role.

Role	Activity	Time spent per month without CRM (hours)	Time spent per month with CRM (hours)	Time saved per month (hours)
Sales Executive	Logging new leads	3	1	2
Sales Executive	Following up with leads & updating status	7	3	4
Sales Executive	Lead scoring & qualification	3	1	2
Sales Executive	Share project details over email or WhatsApp	7	1	6
Sales Executive	Meeting & site visit scheduling	3	1	2
Sales Executive	Inventory matching with leads	7	3	4

Sales Manager	Review sales updates	10	3	7
Business Owner	Review overall sales pipeline	2	1	1

- ➢ **Step 6: Total Monthly Time Spent Per Role**

Now add the monthly time spent for each role across all their activities.

For Sales Executives:

- Manual time across all activities = **30 hours/month**
- Time with CRM = **10 hours/month**

- ➢ **Time saved = 20 hours/person/month**

For Sales Managers:

- Time saved = 7 hours/month/person

For the Business Owner:

- Time saved = 1 hour/month

Role	Time spent per month without CRM (hours)	Time spent per month with CRM (hours)	Time saved per month (hours)
Sales Executive	30	10	20
Sales Manager	10	3	7
Business Owner	2	1	1

- **Step 7: Calculate the Value of Time Saved Per Role**

  Assign a cost per hour to each role, for eg, here we have:

  - Sales Executive: **$10/hour**
  - Sales Manager: **$20/hour**
  - Business Owner: **$50/hour**

  Now multiply the time saved by the hourly cost:

  - Sales Executives saving 20 hours × $10 = **$200 saved** per month
  - Sales Managers saving 7 hours × $20 = **$140 saved** per month
  - Business Owner saving 1 hour × $50 = **$50 saved** per month

Role	**Time saved by one Person**	**Cost of one hour**	**Value of Time Saved by one Person**
Sales Executive	20	$10	$200
Sales Manager	7	$20	$140
Business Owner	1	$50	$50

- **Step 8: Calculate the Value of Total Time Saved**

  Now that you have:

  - Value of time saved per role

  You can calculate **total time saved** by multiplying with the number of persons in each role.

  - 10 Sales Executives × $200 = **$2,000 saved**

- 2 Sales Managers saving × $140 = **$280 saved**
- 1 Business Owner saving × $50 = **$50 saved**

Total monthly value = $2,330

Role	Number of Persons	Value of Time Saved by one Person	Total Value of Time Saved
Sales Executive	10	$200	$2,000
Sales Manager	2	$140	$280
Business Owner	1	$50	$50
Total	13		$2,330

- **Step 9: Compare Costs & Gains**

  The CRM costs $50 per user per month. With 13 users (10 sales executives + 2 managers + 1 owner), the total monthly cost = **$650.**

  Now calculate net gain:

  - **Value saved:** $2,330
  - **CRM cost:** $650

- **Net gain = $1,680/month**
- **Step 10: Calculate ROI**

  Use the ROI formula:

$$ROI = \frac{Gain - Cost}{Cost} \times 100$$

The CRM has an **ROI of 258% or 2.5x**, which means that every dollar invested in the CRM gets you $2.5 in profit.

Description	Option A: Manual Process	Option B: With CRM
Monthly Hours Spent	322 hours	107 hours
Time Saved with CRM		215 hours
Value of Time Spent	$3,500	$1,170
Value of Time Saved		$2,330
CRM Cost		$\$50 \times 13 = \$650$
Net Gain from CRM Investment		$\$2330 - \$650 = \$1680$
ROI		$\frac{\$1680}{\$650} \times 100 = 258\%$

This is how smart businesses calculate ROI:

- Not based on price,
- But based on **time saved**, **value added**, and **growth potential**.

Use this same method for your own business. The Action Plan at the end of this chapter will help you apply these steps.

Final Thought – Smart Investments Lead to Growth

Many business owners hesitate to invest in software because they see it as an extra expense. But the truth is, not investing in the right tools costs far more in lost productivity, inefficiencies, and missed opportunities.

Think about the real estate agency example. Peter could have saved over $17,000 per month just by making a $500 investment in a CRM. That's an ROI of more than 30x and a clear reminder that the **right investment at the right time can transform outcomes**.

Successful businesses don't just cut costs – they make smart investments that allow them to scale without stress.

The Bottom Line

- ➢ Cheap decisions cost more in the long run
- ➢ Investing in smart software generates massive ROI and fuels long-term business success

The key mindset shift:

✕ **Stop thinking:** "How much will this software cost me?"

☑ **Start thinking:** "How much will this software help me save and grow?"

If you want to do more with less effort, increase profitability, and grow faster, you need to stop taking decisions based on price and start taking decisions based on ROI.

- ➢ The choice is yours – stay stuck in outdated systems or invest in technology that takes your business to the next level.

Create Your Action Plan

Don't choose software just because it's cheap. Choose it because it helps you grow, save time, and unlock bigger opportunities. Use this simple 3-step action plan to move from *"price-thinking"* to *"ROI-thinking"* before your next software decision:

1. **Identify One Area Where You're Bleeding Time or Money**

   Think about where your team spends the most time doing manual or repetitive tasks.

   - Are tasks getting missed or delayed due to lack of automation?
   - Are orders or leads getting lost in endless spreadsheets or WhatsApp threads?
   - Are decisions being delayed because key reports are unavailable or outdated?

   Write down the one business workflow that feels the most expensive in terms of time, effort, or lost opportunities. This is your priority zone for improvement.

2. **Estimate the Hidden Cost of Doing Nothing**

   Even if you don't buy software, there's still a cost. It's just invisible.

   - What are the activities of your team that can be made more efficient?
   - How many hours are wasted on manual work every week?
   - What's the hourly rate of your team?
   - What's the monetary cost of the inefficiencies over a month or a year?

You don't need exact figures. Even a rough estimate will **open your eyes to the real cost of inaction**.

Chapter 9

Avoid Software Indigestion – Implement in Bite-Sized Steps

> *"A great system isn't built overnight; it's refined with time."*

Implementing new software can often feel like walking into an all-you-can-eat buffet. When you've invested time, energy, and resources, it's natural to want to maximize every bit of functionality the software offers. But just as in a buffet, biting off more than you can chew can lead to serious discomfort later.

The Buffet Analogy: Don't Try to Do Everything at Once

Imagine you're at a lavish buffet. Just because there's unlimited food doesn't mean you should fill your plate with everything in sight. If you do, you'll likely feel uncomfortable and unable to enjoy the meal fully.

In a software implementation, taking on too much at once is similar. It leads to "indigestion" in your business processes, causing confusion and inefficiency.

Keep It Simple!

Start with what you really need and expand as your team becomes comfortable with the system. This allows for a smoother transition and better integration into daily workflows.

Learn to Walk Before You Run

The excitement of automation and optimization often leads business owners to aim for a perfect system from the get-go. They want everything automated, every process streamlined, and every problem solved at once. However, attempting to implement a fully customized and complex system in one go can be overwhelming and often counterproductive.

Scaling your software usage is just like any other growth process!

You have to go from zero to one, then one to two, gradually moving towards a hundred. Each step builds on the previous one, allowing you to achieve your vision without overwhelming your team or stretching the software's capabilities.

However, before diving headfirst into automation, it's essential to first understand and refine your manual processes. A software can streamline tasks, but it cannot fix poorly structured business processes and workflows. Jumping straight into automation without having a well-defined business process often leads to confusion, inefficiencies, and frustration.

To ensure a smooth transition to automation:

1. **Define the Manual Process:** Map out the current workflow – key business steps, tasks, roles and responsibilities. If you don't know how a process works manually, automating it will only amplify inefficiencies.
2. **Refine and Optimize:** Eliminate redundant steps and sharpen the process. For instance, if approvals in your inventory management process take too long, streamline them manually before automation.
3. **Practice It:** Test the refined process manually to ensure it works efficiently. This helps your team understand the workflow and identify any gaps before introducing software and automation.

Think of it like teaching a child to walk before they run!

Rushing directly to complex automation without defining manual processes is like trying to run without learning how to walk – it leads to more problems than solutions.

Software is a tool to enhance clarity and structure, not a replacement for them. By starting with manual processes and refining them, you create a solid foundation that ensures automation amplifies efficiency rather than introducing chaos.

The Dangers of Over-Engineering

Many businesses, particularly SMBs, make the mistake of choosing enterprise-grade software like SAP that's designed for much larger organizations. They get tempted by the impressive brand, features or smooth-talking salespeople. But later, they struggle to use the system because the software simply wasn't designed for their scale or needs. It becomes a case of "indigestion" – the software is there, but they can't effectively "digest" or use it, leading to complexity, frustration, and often, abandonment.

Another mistake many businesses make is trying to customize everything in the software right from the start. This often makes the system too complex and hard to use. A better way is to begin with the essential features you really need, and then add more as your team gets comfortable.

Smart Systems Need Expert Advisors

When implementing new systems, it's crucial to rely on the insights and expertise of experienced consultants and software partners. These professionals bring a wealth of knowledge from working across industries and understanding diverse business challenges. They have the skills, experience, and wisdom to guide you in making informed decisions in your software implementation journey.

At Orgzit, our focus as software consultants is not just on selling a product but on becoming a trusted advisor. We help our customers differentiate between what their business truly needs versus what may simply look attractive on the surface. Our objective is to be your guide in this journey, helping you avoid costly mistakes, over-engineering, and project failures.

Key Takeaways

- **Lay One Brick At a Time:** Aim for gradual implementation. Start with essential features and add more as your team adapts.
- **Avoid Over-Engineering:** Don't try to make the software do everything at once. Keep it functional and user-friendly.
- **Trust the Experts:** Rely on the experience of consultants and software partners to make wise decisions about features and customization.

Create Your Action Plan

Before rolling out new software, take a step back and ensure you're setting up for success, not chaos. Answer these two critical questions:

1. **Do you have a clear manual process in place before automating?** *(Automation should streamline and enhance efficiency, not amplify existing inefficiencies. Make sure your existing workflow is clear, structured, and tested before introducing any software layer.)*
2. **Are you trying to implement everything at once, or prioritizing essential features first?** *(Start small. Focus on the most impactful features. Gradually build from there. This approach keeps your team engaged, confident, and less overwhelmed by change.)*

Chapter 10

From Resistance to Buy-In– Why Software Needs a Human Strategy

"Software doesn't fail – lack of adoption does."

The biggest reason software implementations fail isn't the technology; it's the lack of user adoption, or worse, only partial adoption by the people who are meant to use it. And without adoption, even the best systems can fall short of their potential. But why do users resist new software, and how can businesses overcome these challenges to ensure successful adoption?

Understanding the Barriers to Adoption

When introducing new software, it's common to face a variety of user concerns. Some of these concerns are openly discussed, while others remain unspoken, leading to passive resistance that's harder to detect but just as damaging. Understanding and addressing these concerns is essential for successful adoption. Here are some common reasons why team members may be hesitant to adopt new software:

1. **Fear of Surveillance and Control**: Team members may feel that new software is there to let the management "pry" into their work, monitoring every action and micromanaging their activities. This fear of constant surveillance can create discomfort and mistrust, making them feel more controlled than supported, ultimately leading to quiet resistance.
2. **Perceived Complexity**: If the software is too complex or not user-friendly, team members may find it daunting to learn and use it. Without adequate training, they can become frustrated and disengaged.
3. **Job Security Concerns**: Automation often brings fears of downsizing or role redundancy. Team members may worry that the new system is a step towards replacing their jobs, leading them to resist its adoption.
4. **Lack of Communication**: Often, management decides to implement software without consulting the users who will work with it daily. When team members aren't involved in the decision-making process, they may feel the software is being "forced" on them, which can lead to passive or active resistance.
5. **No Clear Value for the End User**: When team members don't

understand how the new software will make their work easier or help them succeed, they lack the motivation to engage with it fully. Adoption thrives on clarity – people need to clearly see how the change benefits them personally, not just the organization as a whole.

Manage the Change: The Key to Successful Software Adoption

To overcome these challenges, businesses must prioritize "change management" (the process of managing the change), addressing fears, concerns, and objections upfront. Here are some proven strategies to promote smoother and more successful adoption:

1. **Proactive Communication:** Clearly communicate the purpose and benefits of the software to all users. Share:
   - **Why we are doing this:** Explain the rationale behind your software decision.
   - **Benefits to the organization:** Highlight how the software aligns with the company's goals, such as improved efficiency or cost savings.
   - **Benefits to users:** Emphasize how it will make their day-to-day tasks easier or more productive.
   - **Expectations from users:** Set clear expectations about their role in adopting the system. Additionally, listen to their thoughts and concerns, addressing them transparently to foster trust and understanding.
2. **Involve End Users Early**: Instead of imposing a ready-made solution, involve team members in the selection and implementation process. This can foster a sense of ownership and lessen resistance.

3. **Address Concerns Transparently**: Directly acknowledge the common fears surrounding new software – such as job security, complexity, and control. Create a safe space for employees to share their concerns and provide reassurance through open communication.
4. **Provide Comprehensive Training**: A successful rollout is incomplete without proper training. Offer hands-on training sessions to ensure everyone is comfortable and confident with the new software.
5. **Walk the Talk**: Leadership and software champions must use the software consistently. When team members see that their managers and leaders are committed to using the system, they'll be more likely to follow suit. It's about setting an example and leading by action.
6. **Carrot and Stick Approach**: It's essential to find a balance between incentives and requirements. Recognize and reward those who actively engage with the software, while setting expectations for usage across the team.
7. **Encourage a Culture of Continuous Improvement**: Make it clear that feedback is welcome and that the software will continue to evolve based on their input. This can create a positive mindset around software updates and improvements.

Create Your Action Plan

Successful software adoption isn't just about technology – it's about people. To ensure your team fully embraces new systems, reflect on these two key questions:

1. **Have you clearly communicated how this software benefits both the company and the users?** *(Clearly outline how it will make their daily tasks easier, improve efficiency, and contribute to overall business success.)*

2. **Are team members actively involved in the implementation process?**

   (Early involvement fosters ownership. Get their feedback, address concerns, and provide hands-on training to ease the transition.)

Chapter 11

Evolve or Expire – Software That Doesn't Adapt, Dies

> *"Software is like a garden – neglect it, and weeds take over."*

One of the biggest mistakes businesses make after implementing a new software system is assuming the job is done. But just like your business, your software system needs to evolve to stay relevant and effective in a fast-changing environment. Ignoring the need for periodic updates, user feedback, and strategic improvements can lead to a system that no longer supports your growth or aligns with your changing needs.

Why Continuous Improvement Matters

In a rapidly changing business environment, **stagnation is not an option**. If you're not moving forward, whether in life or business, you're slowly falling behind everyone. Progress is no longer a luxury; it's a necessity.

As your company grows, as technology advances, and as market demands shift, your software needs to keep pace. Standing still means risking relevance. This approach is rooted in the concept of *Kaizen Philosophy* – **the Japanese principle of continuous improvement**. Kaizen emphasizes ongoing enhancements and small, incremental changes that collectively create a significant impact over time.

In the context of software, this means not treating it as a **"set-it-and-forget-it"** solution. Software should be seen as a living, evolving entity within your business, one that requires regular attention, tweaks, and upgrades to stay in line with your goals.

Key Actions for Continuous Software Improvement

1. **Regular Performance Reviews:** Schedule periodic check-ins to assess how well the software is meeting your needs. Is it helping you achieve your business objectives? Are there any recurring issues that are slowing you down? Engaging with key stakeholders during these reviews can provide insights into necessary adjustments.

2. **User Feedback Loops:** Actively collect feedback from end-users and team members who interact with the software daily. They can offer a firsthand perspective on pain points, areas for improvement, or new features that could enhance productivity.
3. **Gradually Expand Capabilities:** As new features or upgrades are released, focus on how they enhance your workflows and meet real business needs. Don't treat updates as standalone features – see how they strengthen your operations. Adopt new capabilities step-by-step to ensure smoother transitions, easier adoption, and real value without disrupting your workflows. This gradual approach allows for smoother transitions, and easier adoption, and ensures that the updates are fully utilized within your workflows, avoiding unnecessary disruptions.

4. **Optimize for Scalability:** Ensure that the software remains flexible and scalable as your business expands. Adaptability is key – a good system grows with you, rather than holding you back.
5. **Stay Updated with Industry Best Practices:** Software providers often release updates based on the latest best practices and security protocols. By staying current, you're not only keeping your software efficient but also protecting your business from potential vulnerabilities.

From Manufacturer to Franchise Owner – Home City's Growth Story with Orgzit CRM

Home City, established in 2012, is a leading manufacturer and retailer of quality home furniture, specializing in designer sofas. With its mission to create happy homes, Home City offers personalized, high-quality furniture from three company-owned stores.

Home City's founder, Mr. Deepak Gupta, had a vision to expand beyond its owned stores by introducing a franchise model. However, Home City's existing operational structure wasn't built for scale.

The Challenge: Navigating Manual Sales Processes

Despite its impressive growth and strong market presence, Home City faced significant operational challenges. The company relied heavily on manual processes, using Excel sheets to track & manage sales information, including enquiries, quotations, orders, and deliveries. This approach led to several inefficiencies:

- **Limited Visibility:** Every store used to track enquiries and orders in separate spreadsheets per store, making it very cumbersome and time-consuming to get visibility for the business as a whole.
- **Missed Opportunities:** The business lacked a consistent system for tracking and following up with enquiries, leading to lost sales.
- **Operational Inefficiencies:** The business relied on completely manual processes tracked on spreadsheets, including inventory tracking and order management. This led to poor productivity of sales, operations, and accounts team members and low efficiency overall.

The biggest issue? There was no standardized system for the core business workflow from enquiry to order to cash. Launching multiple franchise stores was not possible without a structured system, as it would have been too chaotic and unmanageable.

The Misstep: Implementing an Ill-Fitted CRM Solution

Recognizing the need for a Customer Relationship Management (CRM) system, Home City initially opted for Navision, a well-known enterprise software solution. However, the Navision solution was a failure, with the following results:

- **Low Adoption Rates:** The sales and operations teams found the system too complicated and ill-suited to their workflow, resulting in reluctance to use it.
- **Wasted Resources:** Significant time, energy, and financial resources were invested in the project but ultimately went to waste due to lack of usability and ROI.

The Strategic Shift: Partnering with Orgzit

Home City sought a solution that was customizable, user-friendly, and aligned with their operational needs. They turned to Orgzit for a tailored, scalable solution.

With our deep expertise in CRM and workflow automation, we helped Home City streamline its sales, operations, and accounts processes, laying the groundwork for sustainable growth.

Orgzit implemented the following aspects in Home City's software system:

1. **Standardized & Automated Home City Sales, Operations, and Accounts processes**

   Home City was able to:

   - Track leads & follow-ups for each store
   - Track Inventory accurately
   - Automate sales reporting for centralized monitoring
   - Optimize order fulfillment to reduce delays.

2. **Built a Sales & Order Management System**

   We delivered a customized CRM and ERP that centralized sales tracking, order management, and inventory control across all stores and future franchises. This system became the backbone for managing multiple locations seamlessly.

3. **Phased Rollout for Easy Adoption**

   With a phased implementation, Home City's team was able to adapt to the new software system gradually without disrupting daily operations. We also provided continuous training, support, and coaching, to ensure that Home City's staff fully adopted the system.

The Outcomes: Enhanced Efficiency and a Robust Foundation for Expansion

Within a year of implementing Orgzit's solutions, Home City experienced significant improvements:

- **Operational Efficiency:** Automation of routine tasks reduced manual workload, resulting in improved process efficiency and productivity of team members.
- **Real-Time Sales Insights:** Enhanced visibility into sales performance enabled data-driven decision-making and strategic planning.
- **Scalability:** Orgzit's integrated sales, operations, and accounting software system gave Home City a robust foundation to scale fast and expand rapidly with a franchise network.

Key Takeaways for Business Owners

Home City's journey proves that choosing the right technology partner is crucial for scaling:

- **Scaling Needs Systems**: Expanding with manual processes will only slow you down.
- **Phased Implementation Works Best**: Gradual adoption = higher success rates. Gradual rollout allows for adjustments based on real-time feedback, leading to smoother transitions.
- **Franchise Models Need Standardization**: A structured CRM ensures all locations run consistently and efficiently.

By switching to Orgzit, Home City didn't just fix its sales process, it unlocked the ability to scale effortlessly.

Create Your Action Plan

Software implementation doesn't end after deployment – it's an ongoing process. To ensure your software evolves with your business, reflect on these two key questions:

1. **When was the last time you reviewed your software's performance against your business needs?**

   (Schedule regular check-ins to assess gaps, inefficiencies, and opportunities for improvement.)

2. **Are you proactively gathering feedback from your team to enhance usability and adoption?**

   (Encourage end-users to share challenges and suggestions so you can make meaningful upgrades.)

From Insights to Action – Moving Beyond Mistakes to Mastery

> *"Mastery isn't about knowing what to do – it's about doing it, consistently."*

By now, you've understood the common pitfalls and challenges of implementing software systems, along with actionable strategies to avoid them. You've gained clarity on what works, what doesn't, and what truly drives successful adoption.

The fundamentals are clear to you, but here's the real question: **How do you ensure that your business actually puts these lessons into practice?**

Every business has unique needs, and the implementation of a software system depends on aligning the solution with your goals, processes, and team dynamics. But more importantly, **choosing the right partner** to guide you through this journey is critical.

If you've reached this point and find yourself wondering, *"Who should I work with?"* The answer is simple – partner with a team that shares this philosophy, understands your unique needs and is committed to delivering measurable results.

At Orgzit, we operate on the very philosophy outlined in this book. Our approach is rooted in understanding your business, customizing solutions that fit your specific requirements, and ensuring a seamless implementation process. Here's how:

1. **Alignment with Your Vision:** We prioritize understanding your unique needs and aligning our solutions with your goals. We don't just deliver software – we focus on helping you achieve the bigger picture, whether that's streamlining operations, preparing for growth, or creating scalable systems.
2. **Focus on Growth and Scalability:** Our objective is to go beyond implementation by setting up systems that make your business more efficient, scalable, and ready for growth. **Your success is our success**, and we ensure your software becomes a tool for achieving larger business goals.
3. **Personalized Approach for Every Business:** We know that every business is at a different stage of its journey, and there's no one-size-fits-all approach. That's why we tailor our solutions to your specific requirements, ensuring that you receive a personalized and impactful experience.
4. **Comprehensive Support Beyond Software:** Our engagement doesn't stop at software delivery. Whether it's training your team, guiding adoption, or coaching your leadership on leveraging systems effectively, we're with you every step of the way.

Transformation Begins Now: Make the Right Software Decision Today

"The cost of inaction is always higher than the cost of making the right decision at the right time."

If you've made it this far, you're already ahead of 90% of business owners. Most business owners struggle for years, losing time, money, and energy due to inefficient systems – without ever realizing the root cause. But you? You now understand:

- The hidden software traps that silently drain businesses of over $100,000 in wasted costs.
- The inefficiencies that are silently stealing your time, revenue, and opportunities.
- The proven strategies that separate software disasters from software success.

And most importantly – you now have a choice.

Every successful business reaches a defining moment – a moment where you decide whether to keep struggling with inefficient systems or take control, implement the right solution, and unlock predictable, scalable growth.

This is that moment for you.

Will you stay stuck in firefighting mode, or will you break free and build a business that runs smoothly – without depending on you for every small task?

Right now, you have two choices:

Option 1: Try to figure it all out on your own. Spend months (or even years) testing different software, dealing with implementation failures, employee resistance, and lost opportunities – only to realize that the wrong system has cost you more than just money.

Option 2: Work with experts who have already mastered the process. Leverage our proven framework, avoid costly mistakes, and implement a business system that guarantees efficiency, growth, and peace of mind.

Why Work With Us?

We don't just provide software. We provide a growth system backed by strategy, science, and years of real-world experience.

Here's how we're different:

- **We analyze your business needs deeply**. No generic solutions. We dive into your workflows, team structure, and goals to craft a custom-fit system.
- **We implement a system that actually scales**. Your business won't just function better – it will be ready to grow.
- **We ensure 100% adoption**. Our onboarding and training approach makes change easy. Your team won't just accept the system; they'll love using it.
- **We focus on outcomes, not just features.** Think revenue growth, better customer experiences, and operations that run without constant supervision.
- **We stay with you till it works.** Our commitment doesn't end at installation – we guide, support, and optimize as your business grows.

This isn't just about software. It's about freeing you from the daily grind, giving you back your time, and setting your business up for long-term success.

Book Your Free Discovery Call Now

We've given you everything you need to make an informed decision. **Now it's time to take the next step.**

- Schedule a 30-minute discovery call with me, where I'll personally help you:
- Understand your current operational challenges

- ➢ Identify gaps in your current processes
- ➢ Consult with you on the right software systems for your business
- ➢ Show you how Orgzit will eliminate inefficiencies and boost growth
- ➢ Provide a roadmap for seamless implementation

No strings attached. Just real insights!

But here's the catch: We only work with businesses that are serious about their growth. If you're ready to move beyond manual inefficiencies and outdated systems, this is your moment.

To book a meeting with me, scan this QR to visit our website

or reach out to me directly via email at **pavan@orgzit.com.**

Make the decision today that your future self will thank you for.

The right software isn't an expense; it's an investment in your business's success. Let's make sure you invest wisely. We're ready when you are.

Pavan Verma

TRIAL &
ERROR
YEARS OF
STRUGGLE
PROVEN
SYSTEM
GUARANTEED
GROWTH